The Last Time I Saw Amelia Earhart

THE LAST TIME I SAW AMELIA EARHART

[Poems]

GABRIELLE CALVOCORESSI

A Karen and Michael Braziller Book
PERSEA BOOKS / NEW YORK

Persea Books, Inc.
853 Broadway
New York, NY 10003

Library of Congress Cataloging-in-Publication Data

Calvocoressi, Gabrielle.
The last time I saw Amelia Earhart / by Gabrielle Calvocoressi.
    p. cm.
"A Karen & Michael Braziller book."
ISBN 0-89255-315-4 (original trade pbk. : alk. paper)
I. Title.

PS3603.A4465L37 2005
811'.6—dc22
2004021865

Second printing
Designed by Rita Lascaro
Printed in the United States of America

For
Frances W. Calvocoressi
&
John L. Calvocoressi

ACKNOWLEDGMENTS

Thanks to the editors of the journals in which these poems have appeared:

Literary Imagination: "The Death of Towns"

New England Review: "From the Adult Drive-In" (I, IV, VI) and "Having Never Been to Gettysburg"

Ninth Letter: "From the Adult-Drive-In" (I, II, VI, VII, IX)

The Paris Review: "Circus Fire 1944"

Western Humanities Review: "The Last Time I Saw Amelia Earhart"

I am forever indebted for the time and support provided by The Rona Jaffe Foundation's 2002 Women Writer's Award, The Wallace Stegner Fellowship program at Stanford University and a Jones Lectureship in Poetry at Stanford University.

For close friendship and close reading in equal measure endless thanks to Aaron Baker, Rick Barot, Jen Chang, Robin Ekiss, Audra Epstein, Nelson Eubanks, Gabe Fried, Jeremy Glazier, Max Fierst, Rangi McNeil, Julie Orringer, ZZ Packer, Julie Sheehan, and Brian Teare.

Thanks for the love and support of Ameya Calvocoressi, the Calvocoressi family, Gertrude Martin, and the Shaka family.

I would be nothing without the patience, compassion, and example of my teachers. In particular, I would like to thank Lucie Brock-Broido and Eavan Boland for their tremendous faith and guidance; Marie Howe and Michael Klein for setting me on the path and always being there to light the way; and Richard Howard, for his steadfast heart.

Finally, thanks to Angeline Shaka, whose love makes everything possible.

CONTENTS

I

Pastoral

We are approaching the river. Approaching the vast pines and power plants, the place the snow begins to darken to red. Here is the river; here is the last point of our looking. Will it ever be a church again? I tried to count every vein in the body. I waited at the river's edge, watched my breath and the boys playing hockey, the ice-breaking ships still far off waiting for nightfall. I watched our town, the mines and quarries; shale, brownstone, the bell-works not far off and the church our body wanted. There is a story I don't remember anymore about the time our dog fell through the ice, how we stood on the shore as firemen made their way to the broken-off part she clung to. How the boys skated warily in the distance and the men said *Get off. It isn't safe anymore.* How they sprinted downriver, the smallest boy sent back for news of the dog's thrashing and he moved with his head down and the sound of the blades coming towards us just close enough so I can see the sun glint on the steel of his skate. Then he's gone back to them and the men are pulling at the dog, now a rope around her neck pleads *Come home come home.* The lone boy making his way away from us, going out from shore to where we can't see them. So low to the ground, his arms scything the air *hunh, hunh,* I am standing on the shore and from somewhere there is cheering and the animal is shaking and breathing hard. We have never wanted anything but this.

The Last Time I Saw Amelia Earhart

I. *Clem Sanders, bystander*

It was late spring and silent,
beach-grass switched like skirts
of women walking past shop

windows on their way to church,
heads bent beside their husbands
come up from orange groves

just greening. I was distracted
by a bird, which was no more
than shoal-dust kicked up by wind.

I missed her waving good-bye,
saw only her back, her body
bowing to enter the thing.

II. *Bo McNeeley, flight mechanic*

I go back there sometimes and think
about things I could have done
differently, little things, really,

like looking at her when she spoke
to me or giving her my jacket
when she got cold. Things you would do

for anyone. One time she said
the body of a plane was like the belly
of a horse. The whole bar cried

Crazy bitch when I told them that.
My dad used to come home dark
from the mines and beat his day out

of us. You couldn't tell soot from bruises
till you washed. Sometimes I dream
of flying. Mostly it's that she's come

back. We're hunkered under the plane
and she's telling me a thing or two
about a world away from here.

III. *Diane McGinty, St. Mary's Home for Wayward Girls*

Everybody makes mistakes,
says something they don't mean.
He was the first and kind.

He said we should get away.
I guess they all say that
till they're standing on your porch,

fists in their pockets,
saying they can't come in
and why weren't you more careful?

I don't think she meant for it to happen.
She probably just lost control
and before she knew,

everything had changed.
I bet she was scared all along
but couldn't tell anyone

because they'd just say
she got herself into this mess
and had better get herself out.

IV. *David Putnam, stepson*

I didn't want to be there
and she knew it, joked about it,
her sandpaper voice calling,

Chicken Little, afraid
it will all come crashing down?
It wasn't that at all. She was

always leaving, always climbing
up from where we could reach her.
Even at home or on the street

you would look away and she
would be gone, walking between
cars or just standing there not

answering as you said her name
or touched the arm of her coat.
She was already gone. I knew

because there was no difference
between the sky swallowing her
and living in her house.

V. *Doris Luman, housewife*

It's easy to lose someone. Last
week, walking my son to school,
I turned away for a second.

Next thing I know he's in the street
and I'm running toward him crying
because in my mind he's gone,

bones littering the ground
like a plate shattered so fine
you're picking up pieces for weeks.

And it's not just outdoors,
in the schoolyard or the bus station.
You can lose a person at home

in the safest possible place,
a place you could walk blindfolded.
That's why I wasn't surprised

when that woman got lost.
Because it's always like that.
One day, walking through a room,

you realize what you were holding
is gone and you can't find it, even
when you get down on your knees.

VI. *Harry Manning, former radio operator*

I dream she's found me hiding
on a farm along the shore,
and my fault she left

and stayed away so long.
She says she's not mad,
but isn't coming back

because everyone's given up.
Even her husband packed away
her clothes and someone burned

her maps. So she couldn't get home
if she tried. And she doesn't want to.
Then she turns away

and I'm left alone, calling
How will I get home without you?
The whole world tastes like salt,

crows overhead shout, *Gone, gone,
gone.* She can't help me any more.
I'll have to walk.

VII. *Joel Sullivan, miner*

How do you tell your children
they'll never get away?
Tell them their only choice

is factories or the mines,
bent heads or blackened lungs.
Amelia Earhart is a dream

my daughter won't give up.
Sometimes I want to shake her,
tell her what small towns are,

how the coal dust coats your skin
till darkness never leaves you
and the sky doesn't matter much

when you're wheezing underground.
She won't believe that woman's dead.
She says, *I think it's romantic*

to disappear. I bite my tongue
to keep from telling her
she'll get her chance in time.

VIII. *John Larkin, ground control*

When her signal died
I left the room
and washed my hands

till the hot water ran out.
It was all static:
the radio crackling

like shirts on the line,
her husband hunched over,
head in his hands.

Nothing looked different
because no one could move,
fold the maps, turn off

the lights and leave her
wherever she'd gone.
We watched the planes

in the field disappear,
leaving us alone
as evening came down.

IX. *Susan James, high-school teacher*

Matthew works night-shift
and sleeps his way through class.
Camille's father lost an arm

to the canning factory.
She left us to take his place.
I could go on all day

talking about fifteen-year olds
who might as well be forty.
I wanted them to see her fly.

This is the picture I have:
5 o'clock in the morning,
they're all here except Matthew

who meets us at the factory gate.
We're walking. There isn't any bus.
I'm telling them to hurry

and they're trying but they're tired.
I want them to make it so badly
I tell them to run. And then we're there

in the roar, she's waving goodbye,
and we're all waving back.
Even after she's in the plane,

even after she's gone, we're waving
and grinning, all the way back to class
where Matthew struggles

to keep his eyes open,
and Ramón says, *If I was her
I'd never come back.*

X. *George Putnam, husband*

Afterwards she was everywhere:
a map in the glove compartment,
shoes on the stairs, her wedding ring

on the bathroom sink. I found
her house keys by the phone
and wondered how she'd get back

inside. Of course I wasn't the only
one: everybody thought they'd seen
her, especially children

who wondered if she was hiding
from me. One girl wrote,
When my father yells

I hide in the barn. Do you have a barn?
The last time I saw Amelia Earhart
she was three steps ahead of me,

crossing to the other side
of the street. I almost died trying
to reach her, called her name over

the traffic and when she turned back
it was a young man, startled
by my grasping hand, saying sorry

but I was mistaken. *Then* she was gone;
clothes sent, car sold, nothing left
to look for. Except airplanes

which are everywhere now
and take me back to her, turning
away from our expectant faces.

From the Adult Drive-In

I.

The hill, no the body unbroken
By the strip mall's lights arced
Harp of her pelvic bone a mouth

Falling upon it like corn cut down
In a field I was forbidden
To walk through. There are so many

Kinds of darkness: her arms tied
To the bed, the shadow they cast
On the sheets whose brightness

Illuminates the hushed cars lying below.
Dark mouth surrounding the root
Or pressing against an opening,

A dog furrowing into the mole's home
Following some distant trembling warmth.

II.

Following some distant trembling warmth
I go to the field where the drive-in stood
And imagine the women kneeling down again

Their bodies splayed against the night sky.
The headlights on the hill formed constellations
I could trace from one form to another.

What was it they wanted that I wanted too?
Her body laid bare, the small of her back
Sure against the man's hand, my hand

An orchard fire warming blossoms unseen
From the roadside. Her mouth finds the woman's
Thigh, that darkness, and we are all moaning

In the pasture. I am the only one hidden
Having walked here through the darkening pines.

Exogenous

Brought down from pastures
from quarried heart
of vanished riverbed.

Your bones the broomstick,
the schoolgirl's breasts pressed
on the thresher's floor.

From whose flanks comes this world's dark lowing?

Suite Billy Strayhorn

I. Just "Baby" Strayhorn at First

Hard to hear the horn of you
with so many dead children

around the house; your sister
Sadie a "coo baby", cooped up

in a coffin from day one,
brother Leslie boiling

in the brain, hugging the floor
gurgling something, well yes,

something like Billy, but who
can blame parents for not hearing?

This is Dayton, 1915
and between factory whistles

and fevers spiking, the whole
world wounds like Baby: Baby's crying,

Baby's gone. Baby your name is
going to have to wait.

II. *Keeping Your Country to Yourself*

With its black and white keys,
its strings taut as women hunched over

their rosary shift. Keep your dark corners.
The children that died before you lie

still in their beds, skin growing gray as stones
pulled from rivers, sheen ebbing, no

real thing. Let your palm rest on the rise
of their foreheads, let it coax the eyelids down.

Let the name of your country loiter in
your mouth, lingering like steam on forced

openings of hothouse flowers. Love it
like your mother washed her fresh dead children:

kneading, unrepentant as they grew
rigid in her hands.

III. *Billy Strayhorn, Ohio Was Just a Terrible Dream.*

Rest now. It was never real.
The factories are nothing more

than the mouths of horns. You dreamed
the man in the doorway. The slap

of his belt is an upright
bass. And what you took to be your

brother hanging in the cellar
is just a lady dancing. Let her

sway. The miners passing don't know
your name, and they themselves

are just rhythm. Ohio,
some fool left staring at the bar.

IV. *Mr. Ellington Denies*

And you are such a pretty girl.
You make the boys swoon so badly

they want to beat you to death.
Do you hear them skulking beneath

bass-key? Billy, you're no more
a girl than Ohio is pastoral.

Keep quiet is a muscle.
Keep quiet is a city

with all the swing gone out of its hips.

V. *On Transcribing the Receding Body*

Your bones a sorrow
of miners making their way

toward a cleft in the earth.
The rattle in your chest, high-heels

echoing through a city
after the bars have all closed down.

Rte. 151

From the power plant's towers.
From the luminescence of shale
quarried near riverbeds.

From bones of the long buried
beasts of our childhood. Amen.
From each porch door, each shipyard,

the broad geography
of the net-makers forearms.
Hallelujah. From lattice

of trees in February's
hushed gloaming. From parking
lot to bedside. Mercy.

From the Adult Drive-In

III.

Having walked here through the darkening pines
The woman finds her lover in the abandoned
House, some hunter's cabin, feathers everywhere.

She's been running, has been pursued, a jealous
Husband who wants her. Is she afraid? Who cares.
We want the fucking to start. The field is so full

Of hunger that when she bends over the cars
Seem to move forward without being turned on.
Two women moving inside each other.

He's coming for them sure as raccoons in grain
Pails. Their pale skin washes the screen
So we're almost snow-blind. They can't see us

Or him for that matter, huge in the doorframe.
He's beginning to unbuckle his pants.

Save Me Joe Louis

When I was small no one stopped the fights.
A man could beat you till you died,
the crowd leaning in, you on your knees,
maybe somewhere someone says, *No,*

but it's like spoons dropping in kitchens:
enough to make someone look up,
not enough to get them moving.
The ref's just glad it isn't him

trying to stand, shading his face
like he's coming out of the movies
into winter sun, shock of the world
made real again—brutal, to be sure,

but America is like that,
unrelenting, you get what you ask for
in the ring or on the kitchen floor.
Someone always wants you to give up,

shake hands, wipe the blood away and talk
of lighter things. And you do
because you've been fighting long enough
to know there's no one here to save you.

II

Circus Fire, 1944

I. *The Circus Makes Its Way Into Town*

No rain for weeks. Cows hold
their milk in covetous udders.

The river lies still as an infant
in formaldehyde,

schools of harried shad shuddering
on pebbled banks, a rank

reminder of August coming.
Two nights ago fireworks lit up

parched tobacco fields, the sweet
smell reaching for the towns, listing

into factory windows where women
working the cemetery-shift clucked

their tongues, spoke of children
burning the whole city down.

II. *Looking Up*

We were sweating already,
our heads cocked like chickens

gaping at the rain, transfixed
by acrobats on high:

an entire family suspended
from a miniature porch swing.

It began like applause;
first one scream then a thunder

of animals and heat,
a sun rising above us

husking our skin. The backs
of children rippling tides.

III. *"It was like watching the gates of Hell open"*

Looked down and saw my bones
peering out from burning flesh.

Saw my brother lit up
like night skies over Germany,

passing flames from pants to hands
to tousled hair. Went under.

Woke up buried in plaster.
Heard wheezing, crying, silence.

Asked for my sister Eleanor.
Watched the nurses turn away.

IV. *Geek*

Chickens don't struggle
till your teeth close on their neck,

your mouth a darkness hushed
as a movie house before

the picture starts. Their heads
roll like ball bearings—you must

bite quick, the neck screaming
bloody murder, the body circling

its head like a harried
planet. Women swoon but stay

until the bleeding's done,
pocket feathers: souvenirs.

V. *"To Calm the Panicked Crowd, the Circus Band Played On"*
—*Hartford Courant, 1944*

Merle yelled above the flames
that we should play to keep them

calm: "Stars and Stripes," "Ragtime,"
"Under the Old Tree."

Women swooned, children reared
up before melting away.

My horn got so hot I blistered
but played on while people handed

children overhead. Our music
drowned out only by their praying.

VI. *A Word From the Fat Lady*

It isn't how we look up close
so much as in dreams.

Our giant is not so tall,
our lizard boy merely flaunts

crusty skin- not his fault
they keep him in a crate

and bathe him maybe once a week.
When folks scream or clutch their hair

and poke at us and glare and speak
of how we slithered up from Hell,

it is themselves they see:
the preacher with the farmer's girls

(his bulging eyes, their chicken legs)
or the mother lurching towards the sink,

a baby quivering in her gnarled
hands. Horror is the company

you keep when shades are drawn.
Evil does not reside in cages.

VII. *Call Them All Home*

One hundred and sixty-eight people embracing,
holding hands, clutching at what small piece remains

of a mother's cotton dress, a father's coattail,
the charred nut of a doll's head. The calliope

of fire-trucks has subsided, they sit stupefied
beneath the smoke signals these bodies transmit.

In the distance tigers whine, gorillas let out
troubled sighs, the elephants will not depart,

walking tail to trunk. Firemen move amidst the hushed
crowd like schoolmarms, touch blackened shoulders, gently

urge bodies apart, all the while turning from
the smell that hangs in the air. These men carry

bodies of children through the oncoming night—
gingerly, as if the slightest wind could wake them.

VIII. *At Robert Segee's Interrogation*

I am the canary beating
in the darkness of my father's breast,

Ohio's wavering lights snuffed out
but for miners' lamps. They pry

our fathers from the airless wards,
spit them up in huddled packs,

coal-dust worshipping their bodies
like preachers' clothes. He comes home,

stokes the fire, drags me from bed,
my hands no larger than sparrows

held over flames till blisters
come. I will not call for mercy

as my father, breathless and seething,
pulls me toward his world's dark core.

IX. *Coroner's Report*

Every fifteen minutes they bring me another
body: a girl whose red gingham dress is resistant

as a tooth and needs to be removed with tiny
pliers. A sixty year old woman, missing

her hands but whose purse dutifully melted to her
side. I keep time by counting hearses

that gather beneath gaping windows
of the hospital. The clock in town doles out

the number of dead. Clowns cry inconsolably,
bowed over like flowers brimming with rain.

X. *Woman With Parasite Sibling*

When I was young the bee-man came
along with preacher who spoke in tongues

and held the hands that reached out from
my porcelain chest, smeared turpentine

to exorcise the body that poured from me,
my ribs holding the head like a mid-wife.

Some bees took cover at the sight of me
and flew inside the bee-man's mouth,

punished him till he lay flat
beneath his swarming shroud.

The preacher, he did cast me out
on the rocks of Appalachia,

both of my bodies shaking hard
as evening fell and wolves skulked round.

XI. *Night*

They said anything with wheels would do
so Isaac brought our tractor round,

stacked children like they were bales of hay,
burned his hands on their smoking skin.

That night he dreamt a lion came
to steal a calf from our hushed barn.

He leaped from bed and ran outside.
It is a sight I will not soon forget:

my love weeping inconsolably,
bent double under stars.

XII. *Graves We Filled Before the Fire*

Some lose children in lonelier ways:
tetanus, hard falls, stubborn fevers

that soak the bedclothes five nights running.
Our two boys went out to skate, broke

through the ice like battleships, came back
to us in canvas bags: curled

fossils held fast in ancient stone,
four hands reaching. Then two

sad beds wide enough for planting
wheat or summer-squash but filled

with boys, a barren crop. Our lives
stripped clean as oxen bones.

XIII. *Nurse McCabe Finds Solace in Religion*

Blessed are the burning bodies, the broken
backs of children trampled by the fleeing crowds.

Blessed the battered skulls, the seashells
of shoulder-blades, the teeth we sifted through.

Blessed are the mothers, stripped clean,
stacked like sea-wall beneath the smoking alder.

And where there were eyes, parched wells.
And where the tiny toes curled, crushed cinnamon.

We carry the bodies to the make-shift morgue.
They are warm as bread pudding, they crust over.

They stick to our trembling hands. Oh Lord,
how they concentrate, how they whistle and sigh

as they are peeled from this scorched earth.
A miracle, how they cling to their sad kingdom.

XIV. *Siamese Twins: One Speaking, One in Repose*

Before the barkers, caravans, tumult
of elephant and giraffe there was only

a canal of cartilage, a midway leading
from girl to girl. The place belonging to neither

and both, an intersection we quibbled over,
chest challenging obstinate chest. See each

hobbling through our days, turned aside,
as though in a doorway, inviting the other

to pass. We washed each other's hair, took dancing
lessons on the verandah, *one, two,*

one, my sister humming Benny Goodman.
I knew we would never be kissed.

XV. *Six Years Later, Robert Segee Admits to Setting the Circus On Fire*

Elephant men, a woman with a bird-sized body dangling
from her chest—the diminutive head invisible, kept

like a secret inside, his pin-sized teeth teasing the heart.
The hydrocephalic boy whose wax-paper skull rises

from his brow like a hot-air balloon. Don't let yourself be
fooled. This is not horror. Horror is a man with no eyes

who comes to your home, eats your food, bones and all.
Who sleeps on top of you with those deep sockets staring.

Who says he will not leave until you do this thing. So you
do and feel like a new man. Your path is lit by children

who reel and flicker through the summer night,
the darkness held off by the lanterns in their hands.

XVI. *Little Miss 1565**
**The name given to an 8 year-old identified, years later,
as Eleanor Cook. Her mother survived the fire but did not
claim Eleanor.*

Perhaps she knew nobody loved her:
standing alone at the bus stop

while the others nestled
together like eggs, woolen hearts

tilting inward. Perhaps her parents
left her out in the snow

till her fingers turned blue,
wet hair frozen hard as biscuits.

Perhaps nobody ever held her
hand or called her "peach"

or "porcupine". She wasn't surprised
when her family let the flames adopt her,

when they stripped off their singed clothes
and left her nameless, smoldering.

XVII. *Feminism*

The women of Connecticut
send their boys to war,

toil in munitions wards,
coax tobacco from the fields.

The women of Connecticut
are vigilant, wear gingham

in warm weather, cover their heads
with scarves to keep from burning.

The women of Connecticut
form a line amidst the fire,

passing children overhead
like rifle parts, pickling jars.

They ignore their burning hair.
They do not fall gracefully.

XVIII. *Closing the Makeshift Morgue*

In the end five were left;
their battered bodies abashed

under cotton sheets like girls
who sit at the edge of the floor

and are never asked to dance.
We numbered them, said a prayer,

clothed the ones whose sex was clear.
I swept the floor, turned off lights,

drove to the graveyard and watched
men dig. I had not seen morning

for some time and was amazed
to see the world remake itself:

grass growing on the tiny plots,
children running through the gates.

XIX. *Northwood Cemetery*

Hard to see where the pasture ends,
the graveyard begins. Often cows get confused

and can be found grazing between stones
lodged in the ground. On cold days their breath

rises from plots they stand pruning.
Soon a farmer will come to collect them:

a black and white procession lumbering
toward barns, their bells breaking the silence.

Someone might marvel how they make their way
home without once looking back.

XX. *"And were you abused Mr. Segee?... And do you set fires?"*
                    —*Interrogation Transcript, 1950*

Bleating in the root cellar
my brother's broken bones shimmer

like candlefish surging from his skin.
Our father is crawling beneath

Ohio, listening for canaries,
watching for feather flash, his face hard

as locusts. I bring my brother water,
feed him from my hand, leave him.

Father, tunneling toward our cowering
farm, hisses, *Keep still.*

XXI. *Soldiers Home*

There was no time to bury the boys
who blew apart as they charged Omaha Beach.

We slept beneath their cooling corpses,
their arms draped over our shoulders

as if walking home through fields
after ballgames or the harvest.

In Hartford my wife assembled rifle parts,
walked the children to school.

They said the tent burned so fast
my girls couldn't feel a thing.

I marched home to put my family
in the ground. Stood in the shade of flags at half-

mast, preachers littering front porches
like carrion birds. The war is over

but they say the pain of missing
limbs never leaves you.

XXII. *Field Day at Fred D. Wish Elementary School, 1998*
on the Site of the Hartford Circus Fire

The grounds are littered with children tumbling
downhill, spilling out of burlap sacks, collapsing

as they cross the finish line last or pull a classmate
to safety. Teachers collect stray jackets, call warnings

that summer hasn't arrived yet, that one can still fall
ill. Beneath a billowing parachute children sit transfixed,

staring into the wavering dome. When this silken sky falls
they can scream all they want and roll and gasp for air.

And it will be waiting for them: this good safe earth
that's had its fill of fire, that will spare these few.

XXIII. *Circus Fire, 1944*

All forty elephants are spared.
Women and children lie two and three deep,

burned so badly firemen can only whisper
stepping between rows of bodies no wider

than a horse's hoof. Hartford is a small town
and news of fire travels fast. My mother

is about to be born, her mother wants her out.
And if she is afraid, who can blame her.

The sky so full of smoke,
leopards pacing in their pens.

and what if somebody called or came to the door and no one was listening? What if someone came to the door and knocked and called one of our names and waited, their breath pooling on the window of the front door. What if the door had been locked and they couldn't get in and find us or what if they found us

From the Adult Drive-In

IV.

He's beginning to *unbuckle* his pants
And I want no part of it, this geography
Of a town I can feel myself turning from

Even at so young an age. He's beginning
To unbuckle his pants and I am no fair
Game but the shot fired. Am the startled

Waking to the dawn cracked wide. Unbuckled
A word with the gag left in it, my tongue
Stopped short by the roof of my mouth.

He's beginning to unbuckle his pants
And let the held bird loose. I am turning
Fast as flames in the movie projector

Am already gone when the darkness
Falls: a trail of ash blown in every direction.

V.

Fall: A trail of ash blown in every direction.
Breast: Seen through the trees, through the bathroom
                 door.
Held: Hand on the back, in the hair that falls over us.
Open: The badlands of our silent town.
With: held. Withdraw.
Stream: Beneath the screen a reckoning.
Hole: Where the mouth passes over.
Breath: On her shoulder   in the backseat   backlit
No: Vast city, what marvels rose from my upturned
                 mouth.
Spread-eagle: No. Sparrow's wishbone, that fragile.
Desire: Yes, on my knees.
Broken: and wanting.
Push: There are no words for this.
                 O dark barns who will move me now?

Backdrop

And what if the town never existed?
Outside of my mind it never existed.

Here is the house long since shuttered from view:
stripped ribcage of birds that never existed.

What vowel filled the space the square once hugged
like open-mouthed girls who never existed.

And every street I ever walked down gone.
No sailor, no hushed "She never existed."

Remember the name of the movie house,
how in its dark mouth he never existed?

Girls sprawled in the balcony, white skin lit
up like gardenias that never existed.

Me on my knees, her skirt riding up like
curtains on stages that never existed.

No mouth circling the shoulder, abandoned
clothes littering the field that never existed.

No nape, no collarbone, no hard fought, *Ahh*
when her dress fell like it never existed.

No ribcage, no bird startled from chimneys.
No fire anywhere. It never existed.

No letters, no mailbox, no language, no
consonant footsteps. There never existed

a place where my name left my mouth, *Gabriel.*
As though some part of me never existed.

The Wreck

I. *Margaret Fuller*

I'd like to tell you how futile it is
to search for a part of me to carry
home; comb, hairpin, cameo, all gone,
settled on the ocean floor but more
importantly, not me at all, not
what you're really after, what's got you bent
double in the dunes, hoping for any
small thing to hold on to.

I am everything now;

the sand you sift your fingers through, the harsh
wool coat that pools around you, the ache
in your arms that won't stop their grasping.
I am the boy you passed on your way
to the ocean and the expanse of blue
that made your lungs feel thin as robins' eggs.
How you stood and stared and didn't know
where to begin looking. How you stumbled
for miles and slept fitfully on the shore.

I am the world of salt

you woke to, I cloaked your face, chapped
your skin, whispered gone on every wave
and still you scuttled to the water's edge.
You'll burn before you leave this place
and curse me. You'll fill your hands
with sand-dollars, cast their bodies
on the water. I'll clamor and glint in your eyes

and you will not see me.

II. *Henry David Thoreau*

Hairpin, comb, cameo. Is this all
she comes to, a list made as I crossed
through farmlands, cities, factory towns?

Here's what I found instead: a boy
standing in dark fields who watched
my train pass, the way he waved good-bye.

Men trudging home from factories,
not one looking up as the train heaved
and shuddered, *America, America.* I feared

I'd never find her, passed whole towns
with my head in my hands, till ocean
stretched before me caul-blue. I knew

it was over, she was gone and I fell
to my knees, scoured the shore to feel
the lack of her, my hands full of sand-

dollars that I scattered on the surf,
their bleak skeletons shimmering
like trains deserting mournful towns.

From the Adult Drive-In

VI.

O dark barns who will move me now?
I am undone by the flickering screen
By all those girls thrown against the coal black

Night. We, all of us, go back to the field
Scene of a back that went on forever,
The closed eyes, the want that entered us

As we drove by and tried not to look.
How will I ever learn to tell the truth
After the places my hands have been?

It is darker here than other towns, leaves
Burn clear through December. After that
We light beasts of the field to keep ourselves

Warm. Everyone has weathered each other's want,
Familiar as the feed store's smell of grain.

VII.

Familiar as the feed store's smell of grain
This figure seen from the road where the trees
Break apart. A woman straddling the pasture,

Arms white as birches that surround the body
Of cars idling beneath her. I cannot
Tell her voice from the leaves, just watch her mouth

Move, bare as plucked birds in a hunter's
Hands. It's a short walk to the fairgrounds.
I want to take her there, to the palace

Of the bandstand and have it out, music
Of tailbone, tensed hamstring, unrelenting
Chord of her neck pulled back till our eyes

Fill like a screen awash in headlights
As the hushed crowd pushes into the night.

The Death of Towns

I remember I thought it was a church.
When I was young I thought the factory
was a church because it rose
from the hills and breathed.
But mostly because my father left home,
walked through the gates, head bent,
and prayed there and was cast out,
bleary eyed, huddled and wheezing.
And because the waters shone, glistened
at night, and the fish we found on the shores of the
bell-works were boneless, immaculate.

        Because it hurt when he came
        out I thought he was wholly
        well. Then silence and not
        a cry so much as the bell
        grasped mid-swing, an "o"
        starting as it stops.
        I was alone and heard
        him breathing, asked
        "What" and "How".
        And I looked and was afraid.

You never saw one alive.
They just littered the shore,
fist-sized, finless, no real shape.
You'd wonder how they lived so long,
got so big. Some didn't have eyes
and others wore their organs
on the outside, bee-sized heart
peeking through and once a tongue
like a lick of hair. They were still
there after they shut the bell-works down,
after the waters started to clear.

                    Because he was boneless, lolling.
                    Because stumps for arms.
                    Because eyeless, empty plane
                    from forehead to perfectly formed
                    nose. Because glistening
                    mouth, mucus, a pane cloaking the "o",
                    every window I'd ever turned from.
                    Because he was a fish
                    they said I shouldn't feed him.
                    Should leave him, try again.

Sometimes I would take her there
and we would lie beside the shore.
That first time she bled and cried
a bit. I told her about bells,
how it took twelve men to lift one.
I didn't say my father saw a man fall
into the cast when the bronze was
being poured. How his screams

came back to him, how you could
feel them in the floor. She said,
The water shines like bells.

        They said starving takes time
        so I shouldn't stay. But I could
        hear him everywhere, the wish
        of his breath, the way it echoed
        in the bell of him as though he was filled
        to bursting with horses
        sighing and chafing against
        each other. His father looked
        at him and reared up.
        And his sweat was like weeping.

The first time I saw him
I thought of my father coming
home burned and gasping for breath.
How at the end of his life, after
the factory closed, he shuddered,
troubling the surface, his mouth
grasping for any small thing. He'd say,
The snow is so red and Who is that
screaming? He'd say, *Oh God*
it's in the water. He'd say, *My God*
we dumped it in the water.

        Flutter. The flutter of his chest.
        Breath. Birds perched restless on his gums.
        The nurses came in. They'd bathe him.
        It made me want to laugh,

their need to keep him clean.
As if he could even soil himself.
As if there was anything but air inside.
Heart. Somewhere a thimble-sized drum.
Arms. No arms but reaching.
In a dream I named him Hunger.

It took awhile to shut it down.
First the machines stopped,
their heaving slowed to a shy wheeze,
then lights turned off, floors swept,
the massive bones of bells left naked
behind doors and finally the heat
receding, lonely caverns cooling one
by one until the last man made his way
out the door, hand working
the back of his neck, back and forth
through the night.

It takes three days to starve a child,
to convince the stubborn drummer
it's time to go home. He struggled.
He arched his back as though pulled
by current and would not cool.
His tongue licked at the air
and he wept though his silence
was worse and held us
like beasts who are no lighter
for having been bled.

From the Adult Drive-In

VIII.

As the hushed crowd pushes into the night
　　　　What night? It was never dark in that town.

the concession stand is swept by the boy
　　　　White shirt, those ribs like branches of broom.

who is too young to work there, who lives
　　　　I never knew any children. Where did they live?

in a motel on the turnpike; abandoned
　　　　O the poverty of my splayed legs.

cars, topless bars and salesmen littering
　　　　How I wanted the freeway to save me

his vision like Kleenex that covers the pasture
　　　　from myself, fallen in razed fields

like snow, feathers, thrush in the virgin's mouth.

IX.

Like snow, feathers, thrush in the virgin's mouth
It appeared, white against the dark sky. How
Did he know we wanted it, that we'd come

In all weather? A drive-in of skin flicks
For farmers, machinists, salesmen who lived
For small towns like ours. So much empty

Land and the mills shut down, our lives like barns
With both doors blown open: you could see straight
Through. O life before the freeway rose, dark

Turnpike passing thin as a shiv through
The backside of town. Nobody looking
For anyone to come home, truckers in

Back, some kids out for a ride, all of us
Expectant as deer in open season.

Having Never Been to Gettysburg

Sedge grass, Little Bluestem, Bristlecone Pine

(O if this were the worst of it)

Not me, that insatiable lyric, darkening

The doorway of small town beauty

Parlors. Brush grass, Salt Cedar, Big top

Dahlia greening above moldering bones

Who know I've never told the truth,

Not once in my life, my name unknown

To the field mouse, the skeletal cats

Scouring slaughterhouse floors.

I was never sorry. I let the town drift

From view, my mother still humming

With current from the hospital's source.

Larkspur, Prometheus, my unwavering hand.